Shallow-Rooted Heart

Also from Dos Gatos Press

Wingbeats: Exercises and Practice in Poetry

Wingbeats II: Exercises and Practice in Poetry

Weaving the Terrain: 100-Word Southwestern Poems

Bearing the Mask: Southwestern Persona Poems

Lifting the Sky: Southwestern Haiku & Haiga

Circumference of Light, Poems by Bruce Noll

Letting Myself In, Poems by Anne McCrady

Redefining Beauty, Poems by Karla K. Morton

Shallow-Rooted Heart

Poems

by Gregory Louis Candela

🐈 Dos Gatos Press 🐈
Albuquerque, New Mexico
www.dosgatospress.org

Shallow-Rooted Heart

ISBN13: 978-0-9973966-4-5

Library of Congress Control Number: 2018954470

First Edition

Interior & Cover Design:

David Meischen & Scott Wiggerman

Cover Art: *Mapping 21* (Serigraph, 22 x 15 inches) by Larry Schulte

Dos Gatos Press

6452 Kola Court NW

Albuquerque, NM 87120-4285

www.dosgatospress.org

Dos Gatos Press is a non-profit, tax-exempt corporation organized for literary and educational purposes. Our goals are to make poetry more widely available to the reading public and to support writers of poetry—especially in the Southwest.

~ to Michelle Dean Le Beau (Shelly),
the wellspring of my joy

~ to the desert willow, whose shallow roots
hold in rocky soil, feeding a profusion
of delicate pink and white blossoms

The Beauty Way /// El Camino Hermoso

Notes

Acknowledgments

About the Author

The Wayfarer

/

El Caminante

Long May You Run

sad okie troubadour
shambling along
the dust-bowl road

blues man
soil blowing away to
somewhere else

from beneath your
cracked holed
shoe soles

every ballad
every line in a
minor key

quick to laugh
quick to anger
quick to leave

melancholy
orphan in pursuit
of happenstance

Sweetheart of the Northwest

A father and mother
their marriage dying
put two brothers on
the Shasta Daylight
called the Sweetheart
of the Northwest.

The boys were
sent away on vacation
after the family had lost
their youngest.

The train, radiant in red
and orange, pulled by
ALCO 2000-horsepower
locomotives,

was bound between
Oakland, California
and Portland, Oregon
714 miles one way.

At nine years old the boy
and his older brother rode
the track to Klamath Falls
and back.

The clackity-clack muffled
they sat in plush seats
looked out
the full overhead windows
of the dome car
that whole morning

watching
Mount Shasta
the steep clear peak
still radiant with deep snow
in early summer.

The black conductor
passed each boy a pack
of Shasta Daylight
souvenir playing cards

on the back of each
a photograph of the train
snaking beneath the mountain.

The Sweetheart long gone
the mountain abides.

Deer Dancer

i. Ascent

On bunched haunches
rippling quivering
against the tug and hug of earth
on the steep, brutal, narrow trail
humped, sometimes strewn
with talus and scree, lined with
bluebells, red paintbrush, pale
columbine—the deer dancer ascends.
His frozen-stiff brown fur no
longer repels the freezing drizzle.
Cold sweat urges a quick ascent
determined . . . more desperate.
With each upward bound—
guided by metal forelegs
made by L.L. Bean—he
mounts and sways
to pueblo drums: step step
step step . . . heave . . . step step.

ii. Descent

The black, wind-driven clouds
swag then roil Zapata Lake.
Their skirts of swirling mist
obscure the naked rock-spines
of Ellington Point and Blanca Peaks.
They drive the dancer into a
startled, graceless retreat.
Zapata Creek swells. Its rock
fords submerge. The track
melts into fast-sliding mud.
He picks, pricks, clicks
his way, leaning into the deep
on weak, cramped forelegs.
Hail cascades, a stinging maraca
beat. The deer dancer, drugged
with fatigue, staggers down past
lightning-blasted pines. He
collapses to his knees.

Chicxulub

sixty-six million years
before my quick
gasp of a lifetime

in a last exhalation
of geologic and biotic
time 75 percent of all
plant and animal
species died

from insects to the
Tyrannosaurus Rex which

left space for mammals
like me to evolve

on Playa Progreso
I politely turn down
annoying Mexican boys
hawking shell bracelets
and necklaces

close to the
impact center of
an asteroid

which blew
the 110-mile-wide hole
twelve miles into the
earth's crust

with my tyrant
species I lie
under the sun and
earth's degraded sky

New Mexico Goathead

Yeah
I'm thorny
some days
today
prickly.

Don't
want to
pop your
balloon but
I got a
situation here—
ese—

on the
centerline of
Manzano
Expressway
5,000 pounds of
metal and plastics
headed
this way on
Michelin 20-350HT
steel-belted radials.

This ain't
no Nike or
Adidas—
ese—

I could be the
last of my kind.

Hurdy-Gurdy

A college tackle
in middle age
recalls keenly
the snap the
bone-cracking
contact

Another
brother
remembers
ice climbs
in Patagonia, knee-
tearing Moab slick-rock
mountain-bike rides

Another
dreams
bone-cold Black Hills
streams, curved rainbows
hooked and released
from his cupped hands

Men:
burned
black
metal
shavings
ground
inside
out

Poker

Plinky piano, bass, stick and brush
do-WAH backup chorus and Patsy
sings "Crazy" to her lazy beat.
Tonight the Clown Society meets.

Plastic-coated Rider backs rip
purr, frisbee, tap down and skid
tossed or flicked—never thrown—
from supple-quick fingers and wrists.

Mexican pesos clink and roll
into antes, bets, bumps,
dealer's-choice poker on
hand-worked, burn-scarred oak.
Clockwise and counterclockwise
pass cards and the sacred smoke.

Intoned, the poker litany lies
liturgically, in folds or hole cards
hooded in hands, poker faces,
bluffs, boyish misogyny,
cards cut more gently than
a player who passes the buck.

Friday nights—the Jordanaires
drift above them in smoky
wisps and layers. Patsy
cries: *Cra-zy, I'm cra-zy for*
feeling so lone-ly. I'm cra-zy,
cra-zy for feel-ing soooo blue.

Koshare, they discard the Jokers
deal sardonic men's poker; they
bend and fold in stupefying mirth
play Follow the Queen. They whisper

We have the cards, the pesos, the
smoke to wing-speed our dreams.

Smoldering, each Icarus falls, broken.
Aloud, nothing but poker is spoken.

Acoma Corn Dance

Fiesta de San Esteban
Sunday, September 2, 1990

A-ko-me, People of the White Rock
great petrified mesa trunk
A-ko-me, cradle board of The People—
great grandfather pine rises
straight up through Sipapu.

A-ko plaza dust puffs up
swirls from moccasins
drumming a summons that
trembles—down the tap root—deep
and deeper into grandmother earth.

Acoma—throbbing spirit—rises up
up into swaying corn dancers
The People surround.
Up the stalk into heavy ears
music comes: The People hear.

On the periphery homeless flow
around the brown-robed Franciscan
who remembers the mesa—shrugging
yesterday's priests off the precipice
flying them home to Jerusalem and Rome.

Impatient with the ancient ceremonial
outrunning earth and sky—
a glance—to buy or not to buy,
the homeless hurry to, scurry fro
(Unseen among them gray-mud Koshare go).

Beneath Sky City, electricity gathers
to close the circuit: through Sipapu

through the great stalk into swaying corn
out from black corn-silk hair, out from A-ko
wind-blown meal to grow cumulonimbi.

Dance returns the drum thunder
to Acoma, great pine trunk
to The People with dancing feet.
Their outstretched fingers
scatter lightning into the sky.

Paean: Man in the Moon

Apollo thrust Neil Armstrong
onto the moon's face
(at moon-faced Jack's behest)
to take one small step for a man.

But neither poet nor president
put any man in the moon.
Dionysus, the mad Mediterranean
transvestite, has no power there.

Men are skulls, sutured
tectonics. Hard head-bones
that sweat and grow restless
mean beneath the full moon.

Diana tears continents apart
shifts glandular tides and
siphoned Lee Harvey Oswald up
the book depository stairs
drew Apollo's Armstrong into
her arms and pieces of bone
and brain out through
poor Jack's shattered face.

The moon has . . . no . . . horns.
Look at her pelvic wings
ample for laying eggs. Dare
look squarely into her round
face, half-lidded, moist bedroom
eyes, supplicant, pouty lips.

Listen: sad misfit Marilyn
always about to whisper
Happy Birthday, Mr. President.

Extranjero

Old Route 66
haunted by James Dean
behind the wheel of a
1953 Sportsman Red
Chevy Corvette

now Central Avenue
mediated by
the windless stranded sails
of Albuquerque Rapid
Transit's unfinished bus stops—

here I meet a fine-boned
Hispanic twenty-year-old:
a Dodger baseball
cap, bill turned back
paired with a San Francisco
49ers jersey and black
running pants.

Around his slender neck
a heavy silver chain
hand-carved wood rosary beads
dangling crucifix.

I turn towards him
striding directly to where
I sit on the tailgate
of my truck resting after
a Bosque Trail bike ride.

Up close
I see his
luminous
ancient eyes

welling up
fixed upon me.

He slides onto the tailgate,
butts against me, wraps his
sinuous arms around my
neck, lays his head on my
right shoulder—and weeps

as if he has lost his mother.
Over and over he chokes
out, *Forgive me.*
I am so sorry.

Old enough to be
his abuelo, I hold
him close
try to say
a word a phrase
to console.

Chaco Canyon I

It is October
unseasonably warm.
It is morning. Dark Woman
weaves four-wing saltbush
greasewood, big sage
sallow rabbit brush.

Casa Chiquita—
pitted, molar-tooth
sandstone walls stretching
back and, briefly, beyond
twenty generations—pulls
shadows over her head.

Advancing light kindles
the tops of yellow-green
cottonwoods. Fajada Butte
uncoils northwest crushing
cracked dull-copper
leaves in Chaco Wash.

Drowsy, La Chiquita now
throws back her cowl
onto northeast cliff walls
sinks into millennial night
then conjures a blue moon
to fully declare herself.

Canyon—open mouth
cloud lake curved
around your rim—to slake
your parched tongue, you must
wait for snow, then sing.

Archtop

The guitarist
has not
picked up
or cradled his
Stella jazzbox
for months

has not
opened the lid of
her black case
to say
Hello, baby.

She frets.
Her fine
long neck,
big arched box
shaped
like her
little-sister
fiddles.

There is a
complacency
about
the guitarist
this
handsome
black
blues
player
as if

the blues
were not
played on
scarred cheap
Adirondack
red spruce.

When finally he
unclasps
her case
she lies inert
as he thought
she would

her neck
broke.

Angels Are Counterpunchers

Angels never throw
the first punch.
They wear glasses
they don't need.
They turn the other
cheek.

Chubby cherubim
between harping
and singing falsetto
spar with shadows
that always throw
the first punch.

Beelzebub and Lucifer
ganged up on Michael
before his left-right
combination
knocked them
out of heaven.

Then he gently
escorted Adam
and Eve out
of Eden
before he drew
his flaming sword.

Gabriel offers Mary
a white fleur-de-lis
before delivering his
big news: *You are
knocked up. Your baby
is a sacrificial god.*

Incidentally, the lily
is in his left hand.
Even when he practices
jazz trumpet, he keeps
his right hand free
for an uppercut.

Los Manzanos

The passenger jet leaves a quiet
vapor wake across the sky. The
cross-country skier—there—below
glides along, along on pristine snow
somewhere between Thomas
Hobbes and Jean-Jacques Rousseau.

Metal foreleg poles hindquarter skis
chunk shish chunk shish chunk shish
the Acoma deer dancer slides
down the side of a steep arroyo
somewhere between Thomas
Hobbes and Jean-Jacques Rousseau.

Single-seed juniper brown scrub
oak Douglass fir tortured piñon
chunk shish chunk shish chunk shish
he comes upon two old snow angels
somewhere between Thomas
Hobbes and Jean-Jacques Rousseau

then—*chunk chunk*—upon hungry
purposeful coyote tracks—meeting
those of a leaping jack the
quick pivot spattered blood
one carcass half-devoured in
a temporary juniper lair.

There imprinted in deep snow
he reads natural philosophy.

Now in his return tracks
a tingling up and down his back

up the arroyo *chunk chunk shish*
his knees stiff in the twilight
an old buck—freezing
before the ripping blow

somewhere between Thomas
Hobbes and Jean-Jacques Rousseau.

Wingless Moth

scrabbling
over the gray-white
crusted
sinter cone of
Yellowstone's
Lone Star Geyser

a wingless moth
just on the rim of
eruption
tries to learn
how to move

beside crackling
steam superheated
water back from its
five-hundred year

percolation
ten thousand feet
up from the caldera

scrabbling here
on threads
across her
skin he is aware
that

she knows
his trembling
from among
feet hooves
talons roots

Heartbreakers

Along the ragged Monterey coastline
are old torpedo-shaped sea bulls
without a territory or harem to defend,
their large formerly-luminous eyes
compressed to nearsightedness, lenses
dimmed by the multifaceted glare off water.

Leg bones bent and buried in their bodies
they migrate back and forth along the shore.
Look for them in small bachelor groups
or alone: sea lions, sleek black synthetic
rubber in place of silky skin and blubber
trussing up their fifty-something bellies.

Facing seaward in tingling salt-seaweed air
early when the surface of Monterey Bay is
glass, these surfers wait and wait for the mysterious
humps up from the deep basalt and ooze
the rhythm of 500 million years: granite-
breaking waves moving against the land

crushing it into boulders, gravel, sand.
Waves sent by wind, earthquake, sun
moon—behemoths, sometimes from
the Ring of Fire off Japan. They move
through the hula-dancing kelp, orca seeking
the young and the slow, opening their jaws.

The old bulls pivot their long
polyurethane foam-and-fiberglass boards
dig, dig, dig for the shore. Lifted
by the palm, past the opposing thumb
up to thin fingertips, they hear the hiss
steam from the moving, gathering hand.

They grab the rails, lift up their bulk
stand and, god, they slide along the blue
line, jitterbug, cut back and back again
until . . . the cupped hand closes to a fist
and hammers them into the sand.

Winter Solstice Predawn

The cross-country runner
long up from sleep—muscled,
monastic, spare—dances on
ballet feet
quicker than lumbering earth

sprints past gray four-wing saltbush
past stiffly bowing dull-green cholla
and curled-up prickly pear

on a narrow sand and basalt trail
along the broken edge
of the Colorado Plateau

past mineralized sixty-million-year-old bones
frozen in Morrison sandstone.

His ankles grow wings.
His tidal lungs neap and heave.

The Lonely Way

//

El Camino Solo

Spring Canyon, New Mexico

Father, you
launched me
without training wheels
downhill

past parked
1950s
Ford and Chevrolet
family sedans.

Terrified
I could not lean
into gravity's
embrace

arms locked
in place
handlebars straight—
I crashed.

Now
each steep
step down
this canyon trail—

on dark loose
pitted volcanic rock
and sandstone
trodden smooth

on unstable
detached
and cracked
gray limestone—

I leave
bipedal balance
and fling myself
into gravity's arms.

Chihuahua Desert

I wait
for a

variable
thermal
desert
wind
in the
shimmering
heat

under
jittering
shadows
of black
mesquite

listen for
the buzzy
trilled ring
of a busy
rock wren

for the
cascading
arpeggio
flute
of a tiny
shy
canyon wren

Crows

Garrulous
cacophonous, not
to them but to us,
they flap down in October
five thousand feet
from the Sandias and
Manzanos the week
of our Halloween.

They seem unhurried
black snow flurries
out of mountains into my
old pecan tree, to yak and caw
as they beak and hammer
through hulls and nut casings
into the sweet meat.

Their black coats, patched
glossy, metallic-violet by
the slanted, southern
bitter-sun glare,
defiant hungry messengers,
deliberate and sidelong
gawkers, gather here
around my unsmiling.

Crows carry winter
on their backs, chortle
and chuckle humor by
the peck, plan tricks on
the dull and dying,
my piñon and juniper
woodpile shrunken,
the ground too hard.

Dying God

Twenty or thirty crows
are sociably ca-cawing
in the sixty-or-seventy-year-old
Clyde K. Tingley
Albuquerque Siberian elms—
until I step out
of my back door.

Now they pop and
chuckle to warn
their murder of my
fetching from
the garage a small
crescent wrench
vise-grip pliers and
pruning shears—all

to strip the noble fir
of its ornaments
hand-painted gourds
red plastic bulbs
white-light strands
willow star.

Spent needles cascade.
I yank the dying
green god from its stand
haul it out through
the enclosed front porch.

It sweeps the Swedish
crystal candle holder off
grandfather's cherrywood
table shattering it against
terra cotta tiles.

Skull

You find 6000-year-old
arrow- and spearheads
in the malpaís
of New Mexico

some so delicately
worked, their chipped
chert designed to kill
rabbits and squirrels.

Recently, you came
upon a stone axe head
hefty . . . blunt . . . now displayed

on your east-facing window
sill, another human artifact
found among sandstone,
slick rock and volcanic scree

above the four-lane
asphalt of Highway 550
hard by thrust-up
Cabazon Peak
a wind-scoured basalt tube.

Then, a month ago
among the twisted
juniper, needled
piñon and
dwarf ponderosa

among vision-quest
stone circles long since
abandoned—
a human skull:

scattered molars
a lower jaw nested
among a collar bone
a rib, cervical vertebrae.

The arrowhead maker
himself an artifact. Why not
take him home and put
him on your window sill?

The square crowns of his
molars speak of Asian roots.
You find a digging stone
scrape a hole in the soft
soil between sandstone slabs

and leave no cairn to mark
the gravesite. You speak no
words, but you ruminate:

What of this skull
and the brain and the long-ago
thoughts it contained?

And you answer yourself
in the still and heavy
January chill:
Look on the window sill.

You have buried
something of art and
philosophy and compassion.

You found his works.
You found
his circle of stones.
You cupped the crucible
of imagination
in your hands.

Pictograph

in the darker than pitch
no thing of dimension exists
no physical or moral direction
nor woman nor man
no story voice division
no movement or purpose

fire and earth and
water and air call
to each other
beget meaning, loneliness,

spirals, tides and wind
before and after
                causality

earth spits   fire breathes
      snow appears

from the wrinkles of
hands grow
deciduous things:
antlers   carp scales
      red oak   blue corn
                        wings

Cave Bear

Darwin
Freud
Sartre
most
unholy
three

turned us back
into our rat
and lizard
brains then
into igneous
rock

go to Lascaux
the great hall
of the bulls
breathe in
Chauvet among
cave bear skulls

come
away
gasping
a brittle
asthmatic

stand above a
scraped hole
and heap
up stones
to protect
the bones

dream
death then
dream
resurrection
that first long
moment of
imagined
immortality

Solar Eclipse: Conchas Lake

i.
One vulture, suddenly seven, forms a patient
waterspout, a committee snout, that drifts lazily
across this lake of shells to sniff out carcasses.

It nuzzles a human mote of middling bulk and years
who, inflated, floats naked and quiescent on his back
in waters provided by the Army Corps of Engineers.

It snuffles the faint smell of life and moves away
where vultures, now impatient for decay, scatter
as solitary flowers of their centripetal bouquet.

ii.
Holding for a moment against gravity
the man is terrified of the deeps he keeps
at his back and belly.

Around him, supine Tritons cup the lake
their shale ankles shattered, sandstone scapulars
and vertebrae scattered among one-seed junipers.

This jobber of mysteries, between beaks and serrated teeth
cradled in the lap of an ancient inland sea, seeks here
where the Canadian and Conchas Rivers meet, an epiphany.

iii.
He anticipates the heralds of prehistory gathering up
their bones to blow great shell horns, and Eros-like
he waits for the god and the goddess to copulate.

Five hours high, the sun comes nigh his lithe Diana.
Stratocumulus clouds of nymphs, some pregnant nimbi

form a screen that lies between the voyeur and heaven
to tantalize and protect his eyes from divinity.

Through the perfect valves of the clouds' labial folds
Tiresias sees the moon hook the leaping fire fish
now become a changeling, horned like his goddess.
His curved back her curved belly enwrapt, the Chinese sister
and brother, each arching lover eclipses the other.

Figuring Her Out

Just stop talking about
yourself. Don't treat
her as anything treatable.
You are not her doctor.

Watch quietly her
way through space-time
the spiral-bellied
arc of the Milky Way.

You know what lies
beneath the timpani of her
skin: bunched-stretched muscles
cupped joints fatty tissues
blood
bone.

But who is she? a spindled binary
system? the incandescent dark
molecular subatomic
interstices of nanoseconds?
light years?

More.

Bigmouth Black Bass

all muscle
and mouth
they breach
spit and
shake out
barbed
hooks

tangle
in weeds
then
snap
filament
line

Italian
immigrants
float
through the
cavernous
mother
factory

oily grit
rammed
under
fingernails
and between
clenched teeth—

washed
down
huge
gullets by

homemade
red wine
heavy
with
sediment

Nonni
busted their
gnarled knuckles
on GE
locomotive
turbines

their
grandsons
courted and wed
English-Irish girls
above the
Mohawk

on the
bridge
between
Little Italy
and
Becker
Street in
Schenectady

Into the Black Trench of Monterey Bay

The bay's loose granular sand
vanishes. Shelf rock drops off.

I stroke my board, again and again
push through the breakers off Manresa Beach.

Waves gulp me into
their numbing smash and tumble.

A pod of feeding porpoise and
a lone California sea lion hump and dive.

Beside me, brother, you
witness the hammering of

my ephemeral manhood, its poetry
in the saline rhythm of her waves.

Chaco Canyon II

I cannot tell you, my friend.

Let the canyon tell her story
carved by Chaco Wash over
the sixty-six million years since
the Upper Cretaceous.

Let the storied sandstone
walls of Pueblo Bonito sing.

Let the frog petroglyph
pecked high into
Cliff House sandstone
crawl farther on its talons
to croak at the sea.

Let calcite limestone chalk here
squeezed into a few feet call
to Britain's 350-foot Dover Cliffs.

I have ears. I listen
for the ringing buzz of the
rock wren as he bounces
on and around cracked-off
talus boulders.

He calls among the
jumble, a fishing-reel
drag fluted out fast as
black bass take a lure,

the two mating canyon towhees'
buzzy *zeeees* before they

collide and tumble end over
end, then in seconds break.

The usually harsh scolding of
the solitary loggerhead shrike
turns quiet behind its dark mask.

Breakfast Burrito

Down lies
a larded
tortilla
on the black
comal—waits
for hash browns
grated queso
crisped
and melted
by mi madre.

Sweet onions
the crunch of
fried pig
the sweet-acute
juicy ache of
Hatch, New Mexico
chile verde
heuvos—

all rolled and
stuffed
into the mouth where
involuntary firemen
open spray nozzles
under the tongue.

Dust, straw
manure—the
crazy
Koshare
clown
burns down
his own barn.

Rio Grande Bike Ride

The yellow stripes
march by to the right
the unbroken white line
on the left, my legs pump
harder, asphalt and
fat tires hum: shared cadence
for my heart, quads, hamstrings
calves and lungs.

A soft southwest wind
wicks sweat from my
exposed legs, arms, face
assisting my fifteen-mile-an-hour
headway north on Albuquerque's
Bosque Trail this summer
morning in July.

A Cooper's hawk soughs
low across the path
in my line of sight from
the irrigation ditch into
the green cottonwood canopy.

Brooding cumulonimbi
intercede between my flight
and the sun's rays: an eight-minute
nineteen second 93-million-mile ride.

Un Méxicano

~ for Amador Pérez y Pérez
April 30, 1927 – September 4, 2011

These days the wind
shears through
Albuquerque.
Today the wind
is personal:
it tears at my
shallow-rooted heart.

Señor Amador, I
will remember you
until I follow you
as I followed
like a duckling
as you led
through la fayuca
Tepito the unsafe black
market in Mexico City
where Federales
did not dare enter
along stalls hawking
knock-off watches
and jacked CDs

acre on acre
a black harvest
defying whatever
Mexican government
of the day or century.
¡Viva la Revolución!
Viva Fidel and Raul
for whom you named

the youngest two
of your six sons.

Viva wily Pancho Villa
who spit in General Pershing's eye
and whom you favored
over my hero
Emiliano Zapata.

You, Señor Amador,
and your proud
beautiful esposa
the Rose of Puebla
took me to my first
corrida de toros
in Tlaxcala, 1986.

Rosa made tortas
of roasted goat,
avocado and cheese.
We sat, not in shade
but in the hemisphere
of the sun, I beside
your third son José
as we watched that

stitch of thread
a curl of smoke
dance before the bull
that young Méxicano
fragile, feminine
a spare rooster strutting
before his hens
the sand blowing hard
through an unfenced yard.

Sandia Escarpment Oak

An escarpment oak
leans with the wind
scourging disemboweled
western granite exposures.

Ugly oak—respectable
bark but odd elbowed limbs—
is more like Quixote the New
Mexico olive than its Virginia kin.

Its leaves befit a scalloped
scrub holly, glossy and waxy
green, never completely brown
in the now dull winter.

A full dune-pulling moon
peers over the shoulder-
blade crest and rudely
shoves against the

mountain's crippled
and cracked limestone cap,
bends over the tree
that pretends

to be oak and reminds
the dwarf that its
prominence is a gift from
the humpbacked mountain.

Sonidos del Solsticio

Flashing—in painfully slanted sunlight
rattling in autumn breezes
brittle yellow, then bronze—
cottonwood leaves . . . fall into air

settle on Albuquerque's sand, dust, caliche.
Mice scrabble through this cover
seek dens
in crumbling
Bosque banks.

A homeless man inhabits
nearby streets. Trailing behind him,
a stiff paint-splattered tarp scrapes
over frozen asphalt and concrete.

As the cold night thickens
he retreats to
a darkened side yard
dodges motion lights
seeks shelter beneath unforgiving
but safe pyracantha.

Most nights he is quiet, hidden.
But under a full moon he will babble and rave.

Every rock.
Every plant.
Every being
hears the crystalline music of the spheres:
through the long
brutal night
the sound of
returning light.

California White Oaks

Titans, their arms undulate each
decade. In stiff winds, they remain stiff
except for a trembling of their catkins.

Demi-gods, their trunks defiant
against Old Kronos, they know that
bending means dismemberment:

over scores of years in hollow cores
their muscular limbs absorb . . . absorb.

Saints, their supplicant limbs, weakened
by tree centuries, crack from trunks
severed in summer's still night

a martyrdom heard only by the startled voyeur
the philosopher's acorn in his heart.

I have a few friends like
the California white oak.

They taught me the manly
stoicism of the oak tree

the terrible insinuation of breaking limbs
the Japanese love of gushing arterial blood.

Their Blood Comes Up

Longstreet's 25,000 men
raised back and up
a Confederate sledgehammer
above General John Pope's
exposed left flank.
Second Manassas
August 30, 1862, 4 p.m.
the hammer smashed the
5th New York Zouaves

whose uniforms were
modeled on the French:
short open-fronted red-
braided blue jackets
baggy red trousers
tasseled red fezzes.

On came the 5th and 4th
Texas. The massed
Confederates came out of
the woods and rifle smoke.
Union Private Alfred Davenport
remembered, *It was a
continual hiss, snap, whiz
and sluck of bullets*
ripping into flesh.

The hammer smashed.
The 5th New York fled:
Union Private Richard
Ackerman said the
men *ran like dogs.*

In ten minutes the
slaughter ended:

the most dead of
any regiment in
any single battle of
our Civil War.

Confederate Valmore Giles
recalled the red breeches
the blue jackets among
the broom sedge Virginia
hills—some writhing, many
still—colored, torn patches
that put him in mind of
April bluebonnets and red
Indian paintbrush blooms
in the rolling hills among
the live oaks of East Texas.

152 years pass:
more smoke.
I stand on this
exact ground where
my Brooklyn boys
stood, now
patched in
undisturbed
snow.

Their blood—
quiet, braided—
siphons up
through my feet.

El Viernes Santo en el Cerro Tomé

Segundo de Abril, 2010

From a distance, pilgrims—
los peregrinos—look to be
sparse curled hair on el Cerro's
shattered basalt skull. The frigid
west wind, el viento helado del oeste,
attacks their backs and bones
bends certain and uncertain Christians
whips them—como ovejas—up
the ancient volcanic vent.

On their shoulders padres carry
their sleepy children or cradle
sus niños contra del invierno
incongruente blowing across the
just greening alfalfa fields of
El Valle del Rio Abajo, herding
them up towards El Calvario,
las tres cruces.

As sacred molten stones,
piedras fundidas sagradas, well up
and erupt, a few hombres y mujeres
humildes on their knees recount
the final ascenso humano de
Cristo, cantan en español los
cantos sagrados:

Gloria Voz de Padre Eterno
glorious voice of the eternal father
Gloria Voz de Madre de Dios
glorious voice of the mother of God

They sing. Christ sags
on the holy tree.

Estos cantantes, these singers,
surrounded by gang
bangers needled in tattoos
chicas tofes, their pierced
midriffs exposed to frío
indiferente, faces cowled
behind heavy makeup.

Ellos toman su comunión
en teléfonos celulares.
Las viejitas, abuelas
charlan, gossip
about grandchildren
and neighbors.

Voces gritan chicharrones,
rosarios, pan dulce,
offer botellas de agua
complementarios de
Shorty Romero for Sheriff.

Mute, barefoot, flojo
con drogas, a wind-scourged
stoned joven stumbles toward
El Calvario.

La solemnidad y la tristeza
de estos cantadores
among the curious and
confused brings magma
through their swollen feet,
their aching knees—
sus rodillas doloridas.

Ellos ofrecen fuego
to those who hurry before
the hungry wind. ¡O Cristo!
sagging en el árbol sagrado,
mis huesos insepultos están fríos.

The Beauty Way

///

El Camino Hermoso

Beauty Way

for Warren Louis Alva Candela, M.D., 1922 – 2007

Someone removes the
light-green oxygen mask
whose cupped vapors dissipate quickly.
Spitless, gasping, emaciated
you lie on your right side
knees drawn up
a preemie laboring
toward oblivion.

Now clenched, those long and delicate
fingers once banged on the upright piano
or squeezed his tenor sax,
once navigated through packed
carpal bones, muscles and threaded
nerves to pry an air-rifle pellet from
a young boy's hand
(tiptoe, another boy had watched).

You open the fingers of your
precise right hand—supple
fingers that never trembled—and
drop the scalpel onto the theater floor.
What is the word you proffer me
as you excise yourself
from existence, leave
the wound unsutured?

You forgave me,
forgave my refusing
to take up the knife.
You bless me now
with the air you leave

un-breathed. I lean—close—into
your last exhalation. You whisper
Make your own way.

Chaco Canyon III

i.
Canyon winds, they sigh and sigh
against these high wailing walls
that lean into cobalt-blue skies.
Shale and sand and mud lay down
on the periphery of cretaceous seas
to become walls who recall prehistory.
Each hand-placed stone, a tongue,
once sang the solstice for the ancient ones
and now the winter sun goes down,
fills the canyon up with blood.

ii.
At dusk with no singer near
two ravens simply
appear from the crevice
that cradles their young.
Up against hand-carved stairways
fanning the heavy air
their wings thrum, thrum, thrum
to feather the phantom drumbeat
down to dancing Puebloan feet
in deep round kivas.

iii.
Chipped and chapped into fissures,
frozen cliff faces thaw.
Wrinkled sandstone cheeks
draw in the millennial breath.
Lung walls heave to voice
the thousand-thousand-year chorus.
The many-storied singing pueblo walls
recall the patient worshippers
to Chaco, up through Sipapu
to the New Jerusalem, Pueblo Bonito.

First Shalako

The men come down
in twos and threes
to dust-dry Zuni River,
surround and screen
six tall Shalako of the
snapping beaks and hooting.

Up the hill a small
Zuni girl chops at
stacked juniper with
a man-sized axe.
Chimney smoke drifts
east swings north then west.

Long Horn goes to and fro
sways side to side shaking
his deer-bone bag, chants
guttural and low to Zuni
and scattered Navajo
outside Shalako House.

The waning
humpbacked moon
emerges
from Black Rock.

From sub-freezing air
an Anglo slips into hot
Shalako House.
His glasses fog up.
Without jostling,
The People absorb him.

A young Zuni man
gently rests his hand

on my shoulder: *Excuse
me, Sir. Would you
remove your cap?*

I am sorry, I say.
It is okay, Uncle, he says.

The Art of Old Men

Donato Bardi
Donatello:
(spirit of the age)
you are near seventy.

From white poplar
you chip, then
color in Etruscan
terra cotta
a spectral
tattered Magdalene
wild hair uncovered
skull-eyed
knobbed and gnarled
hands held penitential.

Michelangelo
Buonarroti
Simoni:
(tortured genius)
in your eighties.

Enraged you
hack Carrara marble
dismember
the Christ's
right arm on
your last sculpture
the Florence *Pietà* meant
for your tomb.

Titiano Vecelli, Titian:
(sun among small stars)
you approach ninety:

Your unfinished canvas
the *Pietà*
your once vibrant
pigments
go down
the throat
of night.

A bloodless Jesus
sags, his putrid
skin sloughs. You
paint yourself in
as Nicodemus
on his knees.
The Black Death culls
Venetians without
docking at the Dogana
or bowing before the Doge.

Old men you
gave us our humanity
from wood, marble, oils
and flesh—made of each one
a god, emergent.

Donatello's *David*

He looks just like a girl!
squeals the young
American tourist in
the Bargello Museum
of Florence:
and so he does.

It has been remarked
that Donatello's *David*
is androgynous, hardly
the seventeen-foot-tall Carrara
marble of Michelangelo
or Bernini's angry and
arrogant young man.
This boy

his laurelled helmet
more like a festive
pastoral cap
his perfectly coiffed
flowing hair
the complacent smile
on his slightly pouted lips
his softly swelling breasts

his left arm akimbo
his slight wrist
small hand turned out
the stone sling
there—a tiny
opposite to Goliath's
sword the hilt of which
David's delicate right
hand cannot fully grasp

hips vamped forward
and canted to the right
left sandaled foot
casually draped over
the giant's severed
head and, oh yes, the
boyish, pert penis.

The wing thrusting
straight up from
the brute's massive
helmet caresses the
inside of the boy's
right thigh, close
so close, to his groin.

Donatello's delicate and
voluptuous adolescent
melts the bronze of
his being. This naked boy
a reticent and
nascent cast of light.

Bacchus the Butcher
along the Via Chiantigiana

South of Panzano,
once a strategic
medieval castle, lies
old San Leolino church

which, Alta Macadam
tells us, *contains . . .
the extremely early
altarpiece of
the Madonna*

but in the town is also
the Antica Macelleria
run by the
giant Signor
Dario Cecchini

whose amiable
staff each Sunday
market day freely
dispenses crostini
provolone salami
prosciutto and
Toscana vino

while he
simultaneously
booms out
Dante's *La Divina
Commedia* and
cleavers—thunk—
through a roasted loin
of Tuscan pork.

De Sirius

we have no respect
we post-modern
free versifiers
for courtly old Italians

or Renaissance
English courtiers
building sonnets
within known tropes

like the stiff compressed
lips before a lover's
first breathless kiss
like a dying star

the nanosecond
before supernova

Darwin, Muir, Abbey

humanity
names
and
maps
wilderness

but
only
our
bearded
loons

disappear
into
it

Grandmother Nellie

You remove the
cardboard egg carton
from the refrigerator

gently pull two eggs
between three fingers and
thumb and hand them to
me. I carefully bathe
them in warm tap water

then place them
gently into the
boiling
pot.

Despite our care
one instantly cracks
billowing calla lily
tongues into the
small cauldron.

This nascent unfertilized
spheroid, in spite of
rows and rows of caged
sterile, industrial hens
bursts into being.

My Elder, My Brother

Heyókha, had you been Lakota
Sioux, you would have ridden
your pony facing the tail, scrabbled
naked with the wild turkeys in
the hard winter of the Black Hills
run around with a hammer
flattening round and curvy things
(soup bowls, eggs, wagon wheels).

Your genius IQ and partisan
resistance to each of Father's
expectations meant you stayed
back a year in high school, rejected
college, asked anti-social questions
and spoke bizarre truths others
were too afraid to whisper
(I dutifully went on for my PhD).

You collected guns—from the Colt
Peacemaker to an Uzi—drew bullies
into fistfights they quickly regretted
assuaged a Puerto Rican who sliced
open your back because his manhood
was as dangerous as a spurned woman.

You ended up in South Dakota—
so few people (and no state income tax).

You went to Italy, took up-
side down photographs, returned
to create stunning marble floors.
You went to Mexico, returned to build stone
walk-in showers, wiped off jobs like
sweat from your prominent brow

spittle from your angry chin
(I retired after teaching thirty-six years).

You gave me gifts: a blue jay's skull
with red-glass eyes, a Fender guitar cap
you found on the road and jammed onto
my head, Stevie Ray Vaughn's *The Sky
Is Crying,* throw-off stones from your
masonry (that looked like Earth
from outer space) and showed me
how to cast a fly into a trout stream.

Had you been Greek
you would have built stone walls
and stone houses and philosophies.

Labrador Retriever

A catcher of fish
springs
from Newfoundland's
icy mists
into the laps
of British queens
and the fields
of British kings.

New-world
Orion's pepper
ground from puppy mills
comedic Model T's
democratically give
loyalty's absolutions
to please
American masters—
noblesse oblige.

Otter tails stiff
thighs ashiver
hock joints taut
Labradors launch
from dawn promontories
into dream seas
night into night.

Broad forechests heave
webbed paws pound
autumnal ponds.

Jet-black muzzles
snuffle vapors
of kill-fresh blood

soft mouthing
duck and geese lovers—
noblesse oblige.

Steaming coat
massive skull and ears
cocked Napoleonic
fathomless
burnt-sugar eyes
unblinking
retriever of souls . . .

Golden Gate

A full moon rising
above the city of Saint Francis
illuminates Assisi's skyline
as the superstructure
of some anchored dreadnought.

The Golden Gate awaits
suspended in anti-rust paint
made up to please and tease
the sea's corrosive air.

Her twin towers bridge
the bay's voracious mouth
that, night and day, swallows tides
container ships, tourist ferries
and zig-zagging sailboats.

Her finely arched necks,
brows, breasts, powerful
calves, feet and toes
les pas de deux
the Arabesque allongée.

The Golden Gate, riveted steel plates
acrobatic cables and trapeze wires
hung by human hands, dances
beneath the marionette moon
rumbling traffic, tremulous.

Tengo la Cabeza como un Bombo

From one whose
abdominals clench
against life's gut punch

to one who bellies into
the world: Your Andean music
had become, for me, chirping threnody.

Now I hear the dense blue-green
and feathered staccato-red trill
of the quena and zampoña.

I hear the bombo's rumble
the thumpthump of adrenaline-driven
heart valves and storm clouds

the Amazon's mud-flood tumble in the
tuvo the churango's tingle of expected rain
scratching at the sky's epidermis.

They do not *keep* a beat but release
it from cumulonimbi:
rain unto the chapped earth.

Los campesinos make a music that
the studied, stiff-necked Spanish guitar
cannot perfume into romantic trovas.

Fallout

From late March to mid-May
the six hundred residents of
High Island, Texas, share their
live oaks, bald cypress, spiny hackberries
and sweetbay magnolias with
tens of thousands of birds:

awkward roseate spoonbills
red orange yellow and white
great and snowy egrets plumed in
long delicate mating feathers
red summer tanagers, orange
orchard orioles, yellow-rumped warblers

hummingbirds—broad-billed
blue or tiny, rare calliopes
smallest birds of North America
their rosy streaked throats and green
backs and, oh, the
solitary ruby-throat that

averages just under three inches,
a tenth of an ounce, wing beat fifty times
each second, winters from southern Mexico
to South America and every spring
migrates thousands of miles north to the
eastern United States and southern Canada.

These flying specks wing five hundred miles
over the Gulf of Mexico unless a spring
norther, as the locals call it, creates
a headwind—then thousands and
thousands and thousands more drop
into and drown in the Gulf.

With favorable winds they fall out
of the sky into the trees of High Island
the first of tree stands on the coast—
exhausted and starving.

My mate and I migrate to High Island
to witness the pied beauty of birds
and at the end fall out over Albuquerque—
exhausted and blessed.

Ellos Saben / They Know

In brisk autumn breezes
green gnomes dangle in rows:
Anaheims, Big Jims, Sandias.

Illuminated in yellow and green
year-old cottonwood leaves shiver.
Rusted-gold crowns of eighty-year-olds
rattle inside (and thrust above) the mud banks
of the Rio Puerco and Chaco Canyon Wash.

Tiny green slaughtered gods
roasted, frozen and flayed—redentores
en Diciembre: posole, rellenos y estofados.

Los alamos throw off the last
of their copper, bronze, black
clothes, reveal themselves as slow
line dancers in snow. They know
spring will come to Nuevo México.

The Ghost of Tomé Hill

A ghost
climbs Tomé Hill
a volcanic vent
30,000,000 years
old.

A Penitente
scrapes over gray-black
basalt, bleeds invisibly
up five hundred feet
on his bony knees.

Edwin Baca Berry
ascends to mount the tree
he planted in 1947
crowning El Calvario—
to hang between
two thieves.

He wrote
after World War II
of Tomé's Calvario,
If people leave me
alone—it shall take me about
three years to build it—
if 500 persons will help me—
I know I can do the job in one day!

Each Good Friday
the ghost becomes flesh.

Thousands of invisible
pilgrims ascend.

Jacob's Ladder

Saturday on the 10K Sandia trail
we squat and fondle Richardson's
geranium, harebell, the giant hyssop
from the mint family. The white and
purple showy daisy, tiny pink blossoms
of the mountain figwort—all are
plucky after an August monsoon.

But the nodding groundsel refuses
to stand up and open fully to the sun.
The rattlesnake orchid roots in
the shade of fallen conifers, crouching
close to the pine-needled ground and
the demure wallflower, a brilliant
tiny red, is hidden and rare this late.

The busy crest highway parallels the
trail some distance but is quiet today:
On its way up this morning, our carpool
came upon a big laid-over motorcycle
crankcase ripped open, pooling oil.
Its rider safely helmeted and suited in
leathers on this hot day. Dead.

We come upon Jacob's ladder of
the phlox family; we kneel before its
delicate, five-petal, purple flower.
Its opposed thin-bladed leaves ascend.

Cementerios de Nuevo México

i.
Among
Padillas y Griegos
at rest—en descanso—
digging in their bony heels
willing rusty Chevrolets
a nuevos
Padillas y Griegos
who store but never—
¡nunca!—sell them
obstinados
esperando
for Cristo at the judgment
to restore
the sparkle to the chrome

ii.
Chevys sink
onto brittle flattened tires
Chevys squat
on tireless serrated rims
Chevys serran
profundamente en camposanto

iii.
Among
adoberos decomposing
restless, inquietos,
in their crooked rows
debajo cruces pintadas a mano
grinding
with their bony heels and toes
their slowly rusting Chevys

enclose
santos
witnesses—en noches sin luna—
a la resurrección
de caliche a terrenos de alfalfa

Notes

"Long May You Run"
~ *for Stewart Warren* (p. 3)

"Sweetheart of the Northwest"
~ *for Lawrence Joseph Candela* (p. 4)

"Chicxulub"
Chixulub: an asteroid impact crater in the Yucatan (p. 8)

"New Mexico Goathead"
ese: literally, the demonstrative pronoun "that," New Mexico slang for "that's right" or "okay" (p.9)

"Poker"
Koshare: Pueblo sacred clown (p. 11)

"Acoma Corn Dance"
A-ko-me: an earlier version of the word Acoma (itself derived from Spanish) used by those outside the tribe to mean "People of the White Rock;" A-ko: a shortened form of of this phrase, meaning "white rock." Sipapu: a Hopi word, widely used by modern Puebloans, to symbolize the place of tribal emergence from the underworld into the present world (p. 13)

"Extranjero"
Extranjero: stranger (p. 16)

"Archtop"
~ *for Bill and Pat.* archtop: Gibson L5 guitar, first made in 1922. The mature Gibson archtop guitar and its imitators, regarded as the quintessential "jazzbox," were relatively inexpensive and thus affordable for many early jazz musicians (p. 19)

"Winter Solstice Predawn"
~ *for Eddie Padilla* (p. 28)

"Chihuahua Desert"
~ *for M* (p. 33)

"Skull"
~ *for Avelino Marsanich.* malpaís: badlands (p. 36)

"Into the Black Trench of Monterey Bay"
~ *for James Gerald Alaimo* (p. 47)

"Chaco Canyon II"
~ *for Mike Robertson* (p. 48)

"Breakfast Burrito"
comal: tortilla warmer (p. 50)

"Un Méxicano"
~ *for Ricardo Berry, collaborator, Spanish teacher, poetry Puck, amigo estimado.*
la fayuca Tepito: Tepito is a barrio in Mexico City known for its open-air market; fayuca is the local word for counterfeit goods. esposa: wife.
corrida de toros: bullfight (pp. 52-53)

"Sonidos del Solsticio"
~ *for Jim Fish.* Sonidos del Solsticio: Sounds of the Solstice (p. 55)

"California White Oaks "
~ *for Jim Folkman* (p. 56)

"El Viernes Santo en el Cerro Tomé"
~ *para Ricardo Berry y Sheri Armijo.* El Viernes Santo en el Cerro Tomé: Good Friday on Tomé Hill. como ovejas: like sheep. sus niños contra del invierno incongruente: their children against incongruous winter. las tres cruces: the three crosses. hombres y mujeres humildes: humble men and women. ascenso humano de Cristo, cantan en español los cantos sagrados: human ascent of the Christ, sing in Spanish the sacred songs. chicas tofes: tough girls. frío indiferente: indifferent cold. Ellos toman su comunión en teléfonos celulares: They take their communion on cell phones. Las viejitas, abuelas charlan: old women, grandmothers chat. Voces gritan chicharrones, rosarios, pan dulce, offer botellas de agua complementarios de Shorty Romero for Sheriff: Voices hawk fried strips of pork rind, rosaries, sweet bread, offer bottled water compliments of Shorty Romero for Sheriff. flojo con drogas . . . joven: stoned teen. La solemnidad y la tristeza de estos cantadores: The solemnity and the sorrow of these singers. Ellos ofrecen fuego: They offer fire. en el árbol sagrado, mis huesos insepultos están fríos: on the sacred tree, my unburied bones are cold (pp. 59-61)

First Shalako
Shalako: a series of post-harvest dances and ceremonies conducted by the Zuni people at the winter solstice, in which couriers of the Zuni gods visit the pueblo (p. 68)

"De Sirius"
De Sirius: of Sirius, the brightest star in the Earth's night sky (p. 75)

"Darwin, Muir, Abbey"
~ *for Dale Harris* (p. 76)

"My Elder, My Brother"
~ *for Eric Warren Candela.* Heyókha: a sacred clown in the culture of the Lakotas, who speaks, moves and reacts in an opposite fashion to those around him (p. 78)

"Labrador Retriever"
~ *for Roister King Coal* (p. 80)

"Golden Gate"
~ *for Tom and Jean Shanahan (and Ruth)* (p. 82)

"Tengo la Cabeza como un Bombo"
~ *for José Amadór Perez.* Tengo la Cabeza como un Bombo: I have one hell of a headache. Los campesinos: peasants (archaic), farmers, rural folk. trovas: metrical compositions or ballads. Andean instruments: quena, wood flute; zampoña, wood panpipe; bombo, skin-covered, large drum; tuvo, large wood, bass panpipe; churango, a mandolin-type instrument (traditional instrument used an armadillo shell for the music box) (p.83)

"Ellos Saben / They Know"
redentores en Diciembre: redeemers or saviors in December. estofados: stews. alamos: cottonwoods (p. 86)

"The Ghost of Tomé Hill"
Penitente: member of a lay confraternity of Catholics in New Mexico (p. 87)

"Cementerios de Nuevo México"
en descanso: at rest. esperando: waiting. Chevys serran profundamente en camposanto: Chevys saw deep into holy ground. debajo cruces pintadas a mano: beneath hand-painted crosses. en noches sin luna: on moonless nights. a la resurrección de caliche a terrenos de alfalfa: to the resurrection of caliche into alfalfa fields (p. 89)

Acknowledgments

200 New Mexico Poems: "Breakfast Burrito"

Adobe Walls: An Anthology of New Mexico Poets: "Wingless Moth"

Circe's Lament: "Paean: Man in the Moon"

Conceptions Southwest: "Beauty Way" (as "The Pleaser"), "Tengo la Cabeza como un Bombo"

Colorado Poetry Broadside: "Pictograph" (as "Myopia: Blacker than Pitch")

Cyclamens and Swords: "Chaco Canyon II" (as "Chaco Canyon III")

Duke City Fix: "Chicxulub," "Spring Canyon, New Mexico" (as "Gravity"), "Winter Solstice Predawn" (as "Cross-Country Runner")

Elbow Room New Mexico: "Spring Canyon, New Mexico"

Fixed and Free Anthology: "Dying God" (as "Sacrificial God"), "Jacob's Ladder"

Harwood Anthology: "Paean: Man in the Moon"

Italian Americana: Cultural and Historical Review: "The Art of Old Men" (as "Italy Poems: The Art of Old Men")

Malpaís Review: "Angels are Counterpnchers" (as "Italy Poems: Angels are Counterpunchers"), "Bacchus the Butcher along the Via Chiantigiana" (as "Italy Poems: Bacchus the Butcher"), "Chaco Canyon II" (as "Chaco Canyon I"), "Crows" (as "The Crows"), "First Shalako," "El Viernes Santo en el Cerro Tomé" (as "Good Friday on Tomé Hill")

Manzano Mountain Review: "Bigmouth Black Bass" (as "Bigmouth"), "Los Manzanos" (as "Manzanos: In the Apple Mountains")

Monterey Poetry Review: "Heartbreakers," "Into the Black Trench of Monterey Bay" (as "Bay")

New Mexico Mercury: "First Shalako"

Placitas Church Solstice Reading Chapbook: "Ellos Saben/ They Know," "Sonidos del Solsticio"

Poetry from the Other Side: "Sandia Escarpment Oak" (as "Escarpment Oak")

Sin Fronteras: "My Elder, My Brother" (as "Para mi Hermano Mayor")

Surfing New Mexico: "Acoma Corn Dance," "California White Oaks" (as "California White Oak"), "Cementerios de Nuevo México" (as "Graveyards of New Mexico"), "Chaco Canyon III" (as "Chaco Canyon"), "Golden Gate," "Labrador Retriever," "Poker," "Solar Eclipse: Conchas Lake" (as "Solar Eclipse, Conchas Lake, New Mexico")

The Rag: "Into the Black Trench of Monterey Bay" (as "Bay")

Van Gogh's Ear: "Cave Bear" (as "Cairn")

Watermelon Isotope: "Deer Dancer," "Their Blood Comes Up"

Weaving the Terrain: 100-Word Southwestern Poems: "Cementerios de Nuevo México," "The Ghost of Tomé Hill"

Wilderness: Land Untrammeled: "Darwin, Muir, Abbey" (as "Wilderness")

About the Author

Gregory Louis Candela is the author of a previous poetry collection, *Surfing New Mexico* (Crones Unlimited, 2001), as well as six produced plays, including *El Mozo Regresa or The Kid Returns,* produced as a radio play for KUNM. He has numerous publication credits, especially in journals of the American Southwest. His poetry and fiction reviews have appeared in *Southwest Bookviews.* Candela has performed at numerous open-mic poetry readings in Albuquerque, Santa Fe and Taos, often as the featured poet in Albuquerque readings. He has edited six books of poetry and performed with two musical groups, currently with Dog Star as a percussionist/guitarist/vocalist. Dog Star's CD *Down to Earth* (2017) was a finalist in two categories for the New Mexico Music Awards. Extensively travelled in Mexico and Central America, Candela has been a student of Spanish and Mexican culture since his first trip to Mexico in 1970. He has translated original poetry from English into Spanish and from Spanish into English. His poem "Cementerios de Nuevo México" was nominated for a Pushcart Prize in 2018. A resident of New Mexico since 1972, Candela is Professor Emeritus at the University of New Mexico, where he taught literature, creative writing, technical writing, and composition.